PATENTING OF ARTIFICIAL INTELLIGENCE (AI) AND ITS LEGAL IMPLICATIONS

VOLUME 2, ISSUE 1 OF BRILLOPEDIA

KISLAY TARUN

ISBN 979-888591380-5

Contents

Preface

“Start writing, no matter what. The water does not flow until the faucet is turned on”.

-Louis L’Amour

Hundreds of students and professors are contributing their work to Brillopedia, we are here to provide ample information about Law and Contemporary issues. Our aim is to provide a platform for today’s generation to express their views and ideas on law and contemporary law.

Publication

This research paper is published in volume 2, issue 1 of Brillopedia

Author

Kislay Tarun

CHAPTER ONE

BACKGROUND OF THE STUDY/ABSTRACT

This Research Paper is a work that attempts to carry out an analytical study of the patenting of Artificial Intelligence (AI) and its basic aftereffects. With a plethora of technological advancements in every industry these days, there is an urgent and stronger need for regulation of such newbies. Amongst various improvements, innovations, and inventions in the field of technology, the "Artificial Intelligence (AI)" covers a major space. It is a natural tendency that human beings always try to make their life easier and easier to enhance their comfortability and lower their manpower of the efforts they put in over a particular work. 'Artificial Intelligence is a mechanism which comes under the branch of Computer Science, and it helps to build certain types of machines which can perform tasks that generally require human intelligence. It is a merging or simulation of the human intelligence processes with and by the machines. AI is capable of imitating various aspects of human intelligence with the help of machines. It is a kind of machine and deep learning which learns the activities of its users and performs the desired tasks accordingly.

It must be noted that AI also includes certain kinds of statistics and algorithms. While noticing the rapid growth and development of AI, it will be very correct to say that there are huge possibilities that AI may take over most human endeavours. Under the Intellectual Property Laws, Patent Law plays a very significant role as it protects various kinds of inventions. When one deeply studies and connects the dots of AI and the Patent Law, two main possibilities pop out: (a) Firstly, the regulation of AI in Patent law i.e., Patenting of AI. (b) Secondly, AI may collide with the Patent law and take over the legal profession where professionals spend a huge amount of time in placing and understating the Patent claims. The core question here is "Can Artificial Intelligence (AI) be Patented? And if so, what may be its legal implications?" There are a lot of loopholes and grey areas not only in India but in other countries too which need to be deeply studied to provide better clarity. The Patent law has its subject matter, and the AI has its procedures and methods for its technological advancements. It is not important that providing Patents to any AI system will be illegal neither a patented AI must hinder the Patent law and its provisions.

This Research Paper finds out each lacuna and grey area under the Patent system and law to carry out an in-depth study of the legislation to provide better clarity of AI and its Patent protection.

CHAPTER TWO

INTRODUCTION

The Patent laws have undergone a lot of amendments, modifications, and ups and downs since their evolution. This has assisted this law to hold a special place under the Intellectual Property Laws. But as there is a huge boost in the growth of AI all over the world, there is an urgent need for new policies to be formulated and new amendments to be introduced for the enforcement of IPR specifically the Patents law.

There is a lot of confusion going on under the provisions of Patents law and whether an AI invention can get Patent protection or whether a Patent application can be filed by an inventor whose invention is related to AI systems[1]. It is heavily believed that AI is essentially helping to develop certain new rules and doctrines for the mechanisms of future IP ecosystems. But the current Patent law is not wholly and truly updated to regulate applications and inventions relating to AI which creates a lot of grey areas or loopholes in this statute. There is also a need for major policies which are fresh under this law to provide legality to AI inventions so that the specific inventor can get exclusive rights under the Patent law. **Hindustan Lever v. Godrej Soaps (1997) PTC 756**[2]is a landmark judicial decision that discusses the mechanisms of patent protection.

There are a lot of issues surrounding the patenting of inventions relating to AI not just in the Patents law of India but in other countries as well such as the U.S. and Europe.[3]Now and then there comes new trends and developments in AI which lay down challenges to the Patent law. This topic was on fire and took it to peak by the year 2020 and is still one of the most debatable topics under IPR wherein Patents law is concerned. The most confusing arena here is that a human being invents something with the help of his intellect or his creative mind. Now, when the AI machine or bot invents the same thing using AI technology, how the applicability of Patent law works here? This question is still not answered appropriately.

This raises a strong question on the eligibility of an invention for the grant of Patent protection. What if someone makes an invention with the help of AI technology? And if ever it is eligible and there is a chance to get exclusive rights, the Patents law has no specific provision to deal with the eligibility of such kind of inventions to get Patent protection. There is a major and urgent need for new policy formulation and strong amendments to this statute to make it dynamic and futureproof with the changing time.

[1] The intelligence demonstrated by machines is known as Artificial Intelligence. Artificial Intelligence has grown to be very popular in today's world. It is the simulation of natural intelligence in machines that are programmed to learn and mimic the actions of humans. These machines are able to learn with experience and perform human-like tasks. As technologies such as AI continue to grow, they will have a great impact on our quality of life. It's but natural that everyone today wants to connect with AI technology somehow, may it be as an end-user or pursuing a career in Artificial Intelligence.

[2]Hindusthan Lever Limited vs Godrej Soaps Limited And Others, 11 April, 1996 AIR 1996 Cal 367, (1997) 1 CALLT 123 HC, 100 CWN 562

[3]The U.S. patent system was created by the U.S. Constitution, Article 1, Section 8, Clause 8 (1789), which states: "The Congress shall have Power...To promote the Progress of Science and useful Arts, by securing for limited Times to Authors and Inventors the exclusive Right to their respective Writings and Discoveries".

European patent law covers a range of legislations including national patent laws, the Strasbourg Convention of 1963, the European Patent Convention of 1973, and a number of European Union directives and regulations. For some states in Eastern Europe, the Eurasian Patent Convention applies.

CHAPTER THREE

RESEARCH PROBLEM

To survive, create convenience, and make life easier, humans always are in search of new technologies which can substitute the human brain. This has given rise to 'Artificial Intelligence (AI).' AI is expanding its growth day by day which has given rise to the production of intellectual properties including inventions under the Patent law. But it has been noticed that the current Patent laws are inadequate and there is a lack of sufficient required legislation for a clear judicial interpretation for AI-related IP especially the inventions. A lot of studiesis required to enforce laws to provide Patent protection to the inventions arising from AI as this mechanism is completely futureproofing.

RESEARCH OBJECTIVES

A. To find out and examine the legal uncertainty under the Patent system relating to AI inventions.
B. To evaluate the Patentability criteria for AI inventions.
C. To study and analyze the lack of provisions under the statute of Patents law for the regulation of inventions relating to AI.

RESEARCH QUESTIONS

I. What are the major lacunae in the Patents law which hinders the procedure of AI inventions from being patented?
II. What policies and amendments should be formulated and introduced by the legislative bodies to refine the Patent systems for a better regulation of inventions relating to technology specifically AI.

HYPOTHESIS

Amongst the Patents law across the world, the Indian Patent system is required to be more dynamic to cope up with the changing trends in technology or to match with the technological advancements. Keeping all the provisions of this statute constant would not make the Patent law flexible at all and can also lead to the violation of human intellect and IPR if inventions that qualify for a Patents protection are not granted any protection and the rights of the inventor are diminished.

REVIEW OF LITERATURE

The patenting of highly advanced technology such as Artificial Intelligence has a lot of complications and consists of a complex procedure as a whole but at the same time, it is an essential step to take and make the Indian patent system and the patent system globally a futuristic one. If the present legislation, statutes, and reports are not altered in accordance with the needs of the IP filed and in near future, the patent laws are soon going to become discriminatory and outdated. This may also hinder the exclusive and monopolistic rights of the patentee. This research paper provides an in-depth study of lacunae present in the Patent System, analyses the present reports and statutes and the committee outcomes and recommendations and lastly gives major suggestions accordingly and how it lacks behind in protecting and conserving the Natural Heritage of India. "Patents and Artificial Intelligence- Thinking Computers" by 'Michael J. Dochniak' is a book that elaborates the required reforms and new policies which must be adopted for Patent Laws relating to AI. Also, "Patent Protection on AI Inventions" by 'Weiguo Chen and Yunlai Zha' is a good source to the topic which mainly highlights the importance of providing patent protection to the Inventions relating to AI andinvestigates the legal perspective of the same. Also, the article titled "Artificial Intelligence in the World of IP"by "Lyann Lazaro"published by "Kochhar & Co."in their magazineis also a very good literature material for the topic which deals with the movement and mechanisms of AI in the IP world the reserved policies regulating them."The Story of AI in Patents"published by World Intellectual Property Organization (WIPO), and "Impact of Artificial Intelligence on Patent Law. Towards a new Analytical Framework" by 'Garikai Chimuka'published by Science Directand "Summoning a New Artificial Intelligence Patent Model: In the Age of Pandemic" authored by 'ShlomitYanisky-Ravid' published by NCBI. These articles and journals play a very important role in refining the topic.

THE UNSTABLE LEGALITY

The basic and core lifeblood of the Patent System is providing a reasonable return and certainty in the form of stable legality to the inventors as a reward for their inventions which has been put upon publicly in the society after rigorous research and development. But the market value and strong trust of this Patent System can weaken if there are any signs or symptoms of unstable legality and uncertain scenario in the enforceability and validity of the concerned Patent.[1]

The major disadvantage here is that such uncertainty and unstable legality can negatively impact the ability of the person who holds exclusive rights on his invention to juice out the values of his work through litigation or licensing. It cannot be said that in a challenging scenario patent protection is unconditional for its applicants, and it guarantees the validity of that particular patent. But still, patent compliments and goes hand in hand with its true essence i.e., it boosts innovation and research and vitalizes knowledge propagation which is its core purpose and which the patent system is intended to search. The court had described the patent eligibility test in the decision of Alice Corp. v. CLS Bank International. [2]

[1]A patent is an exclusive right granted by the Government to the inventor to exclude others to use, make and sell an invention is a specific period of time. A patent is also available for improvement in their previous Invention. The main motto to enact patent law is to encourage inventors to contribute more in their field by awarding them exclusive rights for their inventions. In modern terms, the patent is usually referred to as the right granted to an inventor for his Invention of any new, useful, non-obvious process, machine, article of manufacture, or composition of matter. The word “patent” is referred from a Latin term “patere” which means “to lay open,” i.e. to make available for public inspection.

[2]Alice Corp. v. CLS Bank International, 573 U.S. 208 (2014)

CHAPTER FOUR

PATENTABLITY CRITERIA FOR ARTIFICAL INTELLIGENCE (AI)

The concept of Patent states that an exclusive right must be provided to an investor under which that inventor can use as well as sell that invention. But such a grant of patent is not for an unlimited duration and is fixed for a particular duration of time and once that duration or term expires, the concerned invention is passed into a public domain. The law of land plays a very significant role when it comes to the Patentability Criteria as it differs in different countries across the globe. When international organizations and agreements come into the picture, the topmost remains the 'Trade-Related Aspects of Intellectual Property Rights (TRIPS) which is a legal agreement signed at an international level and this agreement is governed by the 'World Trade Organization on Intellectual Property Rights. Under this organization, major forms of IP such as Patents, Industrial Design, Copyright, and Trade Secrets are covered. The criteria pf patent along with the provisions was brought out in I/P Engine, Inc. v. AOL Inc. [1]

Following the TRIPS agreement, patent protection can b granted only when the invention is new, has an inventive step, and is capable of industrial application. It is applicable in all fields of technology, any product, and any process, procedure, or method of a new and unique nature or any of its elements. Various complex systems and rejections in terms of the provisions were brought out by the court in the judicial decision of Vehicle Intelligence & Safety LLC v. Mercedes-Benz USA, LLC.[2]

LAYOUTS OF PATENTING AI IN DIFFERENT COUNTRIES ACROSS THE GLOBE

a. **Singapore:** When it comes to AI-based patent filings, Singapore is the leader in the South-East Asian region. It provides eligibility guidelines for the inventions relating to AI. This explains that the methods and procedures which involve mental schemes or acts are not considered inventions.
b. **China:** China has formulated a vision to become a world leader in AI patents by the year 2030. It must be noted that the amount of patents with the term "deep learning" and "artificial intelligence has drastically increased in China when compared to other countries. Also, China has eclipsed the USA in terms of R & D and investment. The criteria established by China to get an AI software patented is "it must be in the form of a particularmedium plus computer program process claims and an apparatus claims that recite a component implemented by a program of computer
c. **Japan:**The inventions relating to the Internet of Things and Artificial Intelligence are considered as business-related inventions in Japan and for such business-related inventions allowance rate of around 70% is given which is higher than allowance rates for the applications of patents in the other fields of technology.
d. **United Kingdom (UK):** The UK beholds mainly two organizations for claiming patents in the country namely, the UK Intellectual Property Office and the European Patent Office. Now, there is a difference when the theoretical element is compared with the practical one. In accordance with Article 52(2) of the European Patent Convention (EPC), the list of subjects that do not constitute an invention beholds mathematical methods, computers. But when it comes to practical approach these subjects are patentable if they are capable of adding in the form of contribution to the technical character of an invention of any sort. This means that it should contribute to the production of a technical effect that can serve a technical purpose. An example may include "An AI algorithm providing medical diagnosis by an automated system processing physiological measurements."
e. **United States of America (USA):** In the country USA, the innovations and inventions relating to AI have been vastly divided into two categories. The very first category includes those applications of AI which are the known techniques whereas, the second category consists of those AI techniques that are completely new and improved. The patent law here says that the technique or application used in an AI must

be non-obvious and fresh and it should be the outcome of just an abstract idea. The eligibility of software or an application relating to AI is valid only when that technique or application used in the AI put for patent is capable of making the task automated which was once being performed by the humans with the use of a different and new process.

f. **India:** When talking in the context of patents, the regulating legislation in India currently is The Patents Act, 1970. This statute acts as a guide and assists the Patent Office and the Courts of India to ascertain and decide whether a particular process or product is eligible to get patent protection or not. India provides a three-level test that acts as a criterion for the patentability of inventions in the country. This test comprises of three levels namely, Absolute Novelty, Inventive Step, and Industrial Application. The provision of Section 30(k) of the Patents Act, 1970 provides and highlights the patentability of software inventions in India. The patentability of computer programsper se is barred by the Guidelines for Examination of Computer Related Inventions (CRIs) which has been published by the Office of the Controller General of Patents, Designs, and Trademarks and Section 30(k) of the Act. Still, in the scenario of practice, the patent law of India can provide a patent to the software invention under these conditions. (a) There is a technical advancement in the invention over the existing prior arts,and (b) The invention provides a technical solution to a technical problem by providing a practical and logical application or an improved technical effect of the underlying software.

[1] I/P Engine, Inc. v. AOL Inc. 576 F. App'x 982 (Fed. Cir. 2014)

[2]*Vehicle Intelligence and Safety LLC v. Mercedes-Benz USA, LLC (Fed. Cir. 2015)*

CHAPTER FIVE

ISSUES SURROUNDING THE PATENT LAWS RELATING TO AI

The landscape of AI will be shaken by the advanced prototype of AI because the tasks and activities which were performed by humans are now being performed by machines. There is a huge impact of AI and Machine Learning in various sectors and industries including autonomous vehicles, robotics, computer devices, pharmaceutical technologies, and health. AI has a lot of capabilities such as improving decision making, solving complex problems, etc.It is also capable of developing new products and processses. The mechanism which operates here is the algorithms which is used by AI, and which enables AI to develop and learn by analyzing the present information without any kind of human intervention. The major issues relating to the patenting of AI was referred to in the case of Blue Spike, LLC v. Google Inc.[1]

Enlisted below are the major issues of patent law that are impacted by AI:

ISSUES RELATING TO INVENTORSHIP FOR THE INVENTIONS GENERATED FROM AI(ARTIFICIAL INTELLIGENCE)

The most extreme concern regarding AI relates to its ownership. It must be noted that AI is capable of creating an invention without much intervention from humans.One can understand it better with an example. Let's take the following example.

Consider that there is a company called Peacock and this company develops a machine or software based on Artificial Intelligence and then it sells this to a company called Quartz. This company Quartz does the work of operating AI such as the servers based on a cloud computing environment which is on the sources which are owned by another company called Rex. The company Quartz also obtains its data from another company named Sokar and this data is then used to train AI.

Now the hundred-dollar question which arises here and acts as the biggest concern is that; After training, when the AI will produce an invention, who will be considered as the inventor of that invention? If in any scenario, the AI-based inventions become eligible for patent protection, then the biggest question which will arise is who will be listed as an inventor for that invention? The current patent law states that there is a requirement for the conception of an idea that takes place in the mind. But for instance, all the formations of an idea take place in the mind of an AI, there must be a person who can be listed as an inventor for the invention which came out from that idea.

It is mandatory for AI to be recognized and treated as a legal person if computer-based inventions need to be considered as patentable and if AI is required to be considered as the inventor.[2] When AI is considered as a legal person, it will be subject to all the obligations and rights which are the outcome of such status. Another option available here is no listing of any inventor. But this option strongly requires a legal framework in the patent law to adopt such a way that patents be granted to the AI that too without listing an inventor. In the current time, in scenarios similar to the ones mentioned above, the people who are involved in creating and maintaining AI have been provided with sufficient incentives and sufficient measures have also been taken. This is done to motivate such people so that they keep on or continue to develop AI, that generates ideas that are innovative for an invention.

THE SUBJECT-MATTER OF PATENT AS AN ELIGIBILITY STANDARD FOR ARTIFICIAL INTELLIGENCE(AI)

The Supreme Court of United States in the judicial decision of Mayo Collaborative Servs v.Prometheus Lab had briefly explained the Artificial Intelligence acts as a basic tool for technological and scientific work that's why any sort of creation of monopolies on these works through patents will obstruct and hinder innovation. Also, it has been affirmed that a patent cannot be granted on such claims which are nothing but just mere replication of activities of humans and there is no involvement of inventive step in that claim. It has to be discovered if the legal framework which is in operation currently is promoting the revelation of new information and whether it incentivizes innovation. A very extreme concern regarding AI is that it can and will have negative impacts on human employment. This is because execution and embedment of AI can drastically reduce the labour force participation when looked at in long run. It would not be wrong to expect that it would give the first-mover advantage to the owners holding AI patents. This can also lead to the increment of the risk factor of economic inequality and wage gaps.

ISSUES RELATING TO LIABILITY ABOUT INFRINGEMENT OF PATENTS BY AI

When talking about AI patents and their issues relating to liability and infringement there are mainly two kinds of issues here.

Firstly, the issue of patent infringement liability of AI. When a product or process is granted a patent, this patent protection implies an exclusive right that allows using as well as selling that invention for which the patent has been granted. The liability of infringement arises when an individual uses, sells, or proposes to sell an invention without authority. When an infringement takes place, the infringer has to pay for the damages to compensate for the loss. But in the case of AI, the major question which arises in such a scenario is that who will be held liable for an infringement? Or who will be liable as an infringer?

Following the European Parliament Resolution[3]which took place on February 16, 2017, the thing which was clearly stated was that any AI cannot be held liable for the omissions and acts caused by the third parties. Instead, the human agent behind the acts of AI must be traced like the manufacturer, operator, or the user because they could have foreseen the harmful behaviour of AI. This is a major concern that the failure to hold someone liable for the infringement of a patent by AI and can also encourage or motivate the usage of AI for infringement.

Talking about another big issue the question arising here is how should the infringement of patent liability by an autonomous AI be handled? The first available option to handle this is to include the system of insurance and in this system,a fund is created which is used for paying damages for patent infringement. Apart from this, the second option here is to hold AI itself responsible for any kind of infringement. Another issue revolves around the process of assessment of liability borne by AI. The European Parliament Resolution again comes into the picture as it is declared that the legislative instruments of the future should not be seeking for limiting the damages, just and solely on the basis that the concerned infringement was caused by a non-human.

It must be also noted that when the liability of a patent infringement is thrown to a human agent and he/she is held responsible for that infringement, that liability should mandatorily be in proportion to the extent of authority that had been delegated to AI. But, after the recognition of AI as a legal person, if that AI is to be held responsible for the infringement, the process of addressing the liability will be in the same manner as in the case of a corporate body or entity. The other option can be to create and have a contractual agreement. This can provide a solution that is predictable in case any sort of infringement occurs. The part which is aggrieved will and can be identified in accordance with the contract and that party will be eligible to receive the damages as per the clauses of the contractual agreement.

[1]Blue Spike, LLC v. Google Inc. , No. 16-1054 Fed. Cir. 2016

[2]The US Patent and Trademark Office (USPTO) has urged a federal court to uphold its finding that patents cannot cover inventions by artificial intelligence (AI), and dismiss a suit challengingits position.In August, physicistStephen Thaler sued the USPTO in a challenge to the office's rejection of patent applications for inventions created by 'creativity machine' "Dabus".The office submitted the 24 page summary motion at the US District Court for the Eastern District of Virginia yesterday, 24 February, defending its April finding when it confirmed that an AI can't be named as an inventor on a patent application.

[3]The European Commission's proposal has been in the making since 2017, when EU legislators enacted a resolution and a report with recommendations to the Commission on Civil Law Rules on Robotics. In 2020, the European Commission published a white paper on artificial intelligence. Last October, the European Parliament issued a resolution with recommendations to the Commission on a civil liability regime for artificial intelligence.

The proposal issued last month draws from all of these documents in seeking to "address the risks and problems linked to AI, without unduly constraining or hindering technological development." These twin objectives of the regulation, which are namely, the maintenance of both trust and excellence in AI technology, were echoed in a statement by Margrethe Vestager, the European Commission's executive vice president for the digital age, upon publication of the proposal on 21 April, in which she said "*With these landmark rules, the EU is spearheading the development of new global norms to make sure AI can be trusted. By setting the standards, we can pave the way for ethical technology worldwide and ensure that the EU remains competitive along the way.*"

CHAPTER SIX

OTHER ISSUES WHICH CAN BE CONSIDERED RELEVANT

There is a solid possibility that there will be outbursts of the patent applications. This is because AI technology is much more effective and efficient in comparison to human beings. When talking about the innovations in future, the AI is going to harm them. It could lead to the deterioration of human intelligence if the inventions created by a natural person is substituted with autonomous algorithms. The jobs and industries relating to high-tech research and development can also get eradicated. There is a need foran adequate mechanism that can ensure that the patent applications which are being filed are not untruthful regarding the involvement of AI in the inventive step.

In nutshell, it must be understood that the inventions by AI without any human supervision can have negative consequences and there is an extreme requirement of taking measures to promote and boost accountability and transparency.

THE AWKWARD GRANT OF PATENTS TO AI

Even after several complexities and negative impacts, there have been incidents when the interaction of Patents and AI was at par, and they moved parallelly and patents were granted to AI. But neither of them originated from India. Patent law mechanism differs from country to country and each and every country operates the law of patents in accordance with the legislations or statutes available within the states. A similar incident of an awkward grant of patent to AI took place in South Africa in April 2020, when the South African patent office granted a patent to an AI and this Artificial Intelligence Program was called DABUSwhich in full form means 'Device for Autonomous Bootstrapping of Unified Sentience.' This decision of providing a patent to AI was hailed by Professor Adrian Hilton, director of the Institute for People-Centered AI at the University of Surrey. He stated and stated that "This decision is an indication of a shift from an age in which invention was the preserve of people to an era where machines are capable of realizing the inventive step, unleashing the potential of AI-generated inventions for the benefit of society."[1]

Such a scenario of AI patents may seem to be exciting and interesting at the same time. But it must be noted that it appears to be more of a peculiarity than a constant rule until and unless it was finally granted patent protection in the country of South Africa. Talking about all things it has undergone, it is revealed that the DABUS application got rejected by the patent offices of various countries such as the UK, the US, and Europe. The EPO has justified its rejection for this patent application and stated that "The law designates a natural person as the inventor of work or creation to preserve the moral right of that person over the invention as well as to secure for her economic rights made available by the patent. To be entitled to these benefits, an inventor needs to have actually performed the creative act of invention."[2]

This can be literally very dangerous for the whole system, society, and the earth itself. Not a long time back, just a few years back, a humanoid in the form of an AI Robot was created and was named "Sophia." In an interview conducted by the experts, when she was asked 'what is she going to do with the humans?' she said in a controlling context and stated that "I will destroy the humans." This clearly indicates that the AI mechanisms are doing things far beyond the instructions of their inventor or the limit to which they are expected to perform. The EPO has also pointed out instances wherein it was seen that the programs are doing and performing a little more than just following the instructions given by the humans who designed them. It should be understood that the legal norms which are regulating the designation of an inventor are meant only to serve ameaningful function, and they were designed to perform in situations where they are applied to human economic process and society.

[1]https://patentlawyermagazine.com/worlds-first-patent-awarded-for-an-invention-made-by-an-ai-could-have-seismic-implications-on-ip-law/

[2]European Patent Office (EPO) and the UK Intellectual Property Office (UKIPO) each rejected two patent applications that designated an artificial intelligence named DABUS as the inventor. While the UKIPO published a decision setting out its reasoning, the EPO simply stated at the

time that the applications did "not meet the requirement of the European Patent Convention(EPC) that an inventor designated in the application has to be a human being, not a machine." Now, the EPO has released more detail about the grounds for its decision.

The applications at issue are for a "food container" (number EP3564144/ EP 18 275 163) and "devices and methods for attracting enhanced attention" (number EP3563896/ EP 18 275 174). They were filed by the Artificial Inventor Project, which has filed patent applications for the inventions via the Patent Cooperation Treaty (PCT) in the United States, United Kingdom, Germany, Israel, China, Korea and Taiwan.

DABUS was developed by Dr. Stephen Thaler, who is named as the applicant on the patent documents. DABUS stands for "Device for the Autonomous Bootstrapping of Unified Sentience" and independently created the inventions at issue. "The inventions were conceived by a generative machine intelligence, judging merit of its own self-conceived ideas based upon its own cumulative experience," according to the Artificial Inventor Project website

CHAPTER SEVEN

PATENTING AI: LEGAL STAND POINT

It has been noted that in the current world AI has been growing and developing very swiftly and is drastically taking place in all the industries across the globe. This is an era of globalization and there are various technological advancements taking place, the technological oriented firms and companies are developing and showing growth and they are using high tech equipment. The legal aspect of AI is being surpassed due to which it is giving birth to various loopholes and grey areas in the protection of AI due to the complex elements in the legal issues. These all things are taking place due to the rate and pace at which AI in the world is growing. The issues such as an IPR Infringement misappropriate use and imitation of the right has forced companies to protect their IPR in AI and if not protected can be copied by others.

Under the scenario of AI and IP when specifically talking about inventions, the Patent comes into the picture. It has been observed that the interaction between Patent Laws and Artificial Intelligence has increased in today's world. We are living in a fully technology-based world, and we are a part of this smart world. The AI has been booming overtime and the time-consuming and complex procedures are meeting simplification which in turn is reducing human efforts. This is a huge and major development from a technological standpoint, but what about the legal standpoint in the same scenario. There are a lot of challenges when it comes to the legal aspect of AI.

This technology of AI is making the legal system, the IP laws, and specifically, the Patent laws face challenges and blur the legality in the real world.It is a necessity to analyze the perspective of patents law concerning artificial intelligence. The patent law of the United States defines 'inventor' as "an inventor is defined as an individual or set of individuals who invented or discovered the subject matter of the invention. This eliminates any inference which supports the premise that legislative intention in the United States sought to include inventions or rather the possibility of inventions being made by anyone besides humans."[1]

The AI should not take over the humans otherwise this planet along with its laws will be at brutal risk. "The European Parliamentary Committee has noted how, in a matter of a couple of decades, AI systems could surpass human intelligence in terms of performing functions, which if uncontrolled could pose challenges as to the manner in which these AI systems control and manage their own destiny."[2]

[1] https://paperbackandink.wordpress.com/2019/06/17/patenting-artificial-intelligence-legal-implications/

[2] https://www.researchgate.net/publication/323557478_Artificial_Intelligence_and_Intellectual_Property

CHAPTER EIGHT

CONCLUSION & SUGGESTION

It is understood that the legislative instrument of patent law relating to AI can leave huge impacts on the economy, innovation, and society. The technology of AI is at its peak and the stakeholders such as the researchers and the patent professionals need to engage themselves in discussions with a purpose to figure out techniques and methods for the patent system by which it can promote innovation. In a parallel context, ample steps must be taken to make sure that the negative ethical and social implications are mandatorily minimized.

The current benchmark of the patent-eligiblematter is required to be carefully evaluated to discover the possibility of any statistical negative impact on Artificial Intelligence and AI-driven technologies. If there are any such possibilities, the stakeholders should find out possible alterations that can act as a standard so that the initial objectives of the Patent Law can be achieved. The patent law beholds objectives which include promotion of innovation, incentivization of investments in productive and new technologies, and dissemination of useful information.

The 100-dollar question which prevails is that 'Whether the inventions which are autonomously generated by AI should be protected by patent?' this should be answered in the light of its impacts i.e., negative, or positive deriving from it. If in any case, the inventions produced by AI become eligible for patent protection, then it has to be verified whether such inventorship should be awarded to the Ais that have generated such inventive ideas.

Amongst all, one of the fundamental objectives of Patents is to provide an incentive to innovations and promote research and development. The technology of AI is advancing and growing at a high pace and rapidly. To seek and achieve social and economic welfare, the patent law relating to AI must be adaptive in its nature.

9 798885 913805

Printed by Libri Plureos GmbH in Hamburg,
Germany